My Dog:
The Paradox

Other books by

The Oatmeal

- *How to Tell If Your Cat Is Plotting to Kill You*

- *5 Very Good Reasons to Punch a Dolphin in the Mouth (And Other Useful Guides)*

My Dog:
The Paradox

A Lovable Discourse about Man's Best Friend

The Oatmeal

Andrews McMeel
Publishing, LLC

Kansas City • Sydney • London

Introduction

"Every pet is a tiny tragedy waiting to happen."
–George Carlin

Several years ago, I adopted a small bearlike creature and named him Rambo. This lovable, impulsive animal soon became quite precious to me, and I got to work right away on convincing myself that he was immortal and would live for many thousands of years. I couldn't stand the idea that my dog had an expiration date that was roughly the equivalent of three and a half presidential terms.

"It just occurred to me that my dog has no idea what my name is," a friend once told me. I thought about this for weeks. A dog is man's best friend, but what is man to a dog? What does he think of me, this towering apelike mammal who showers him with snacks, massages, and love? Are our feelings mutual? Does he like me as much as I like him? I tried asking him once and he responded by licking his balls.

My dog is not afraid of grizzly bears, but the vacuum scares the crap out of him. He won't eat broccoli, but he'll happily feast on dried cat turds. He trembles in fear if he sees me holding a bottle of dog shampoo, but he'd fearlessly sprint across the freeway if there was a squirrel on the other side.

These thoughts all culminated into "My Dog: The Paradox," and they lived in my notebook for several years as a jumbled collection of ideas and scribbles about man's best friend. I originally wrote this comic as a funny look at the illogical fears of dogs, but it ended up becoming a meditation on their reckless, impulsive, and completely lovable mortality.

This book is dedicated to all the dogs I've owned (or lived with), including Rambo, Beatrix, Arnold, Teddy, Nanuk, Donald, Bubba, Rosie, Lori, Chip, Barbara Walters, and Coconut.

But mostly, it's dedicated to Rambo.

My dog does not fear automobiles, garbage trucks, or airplanes

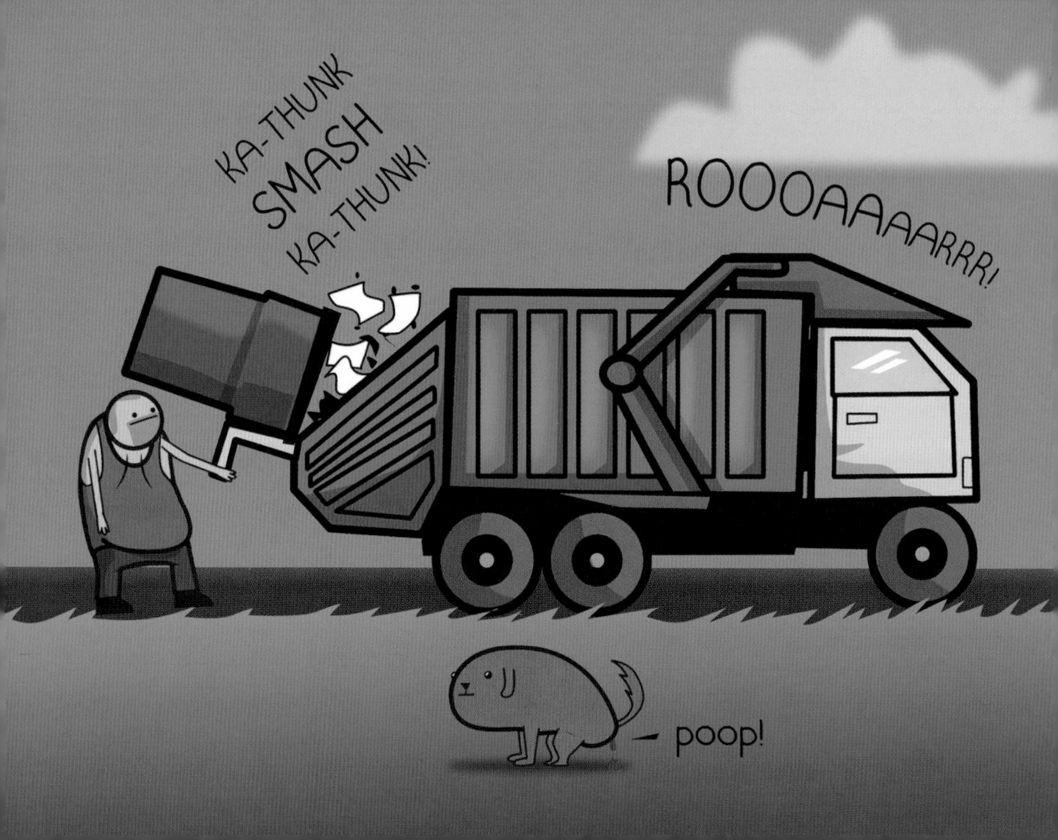
KA-THUNK
SMASH
KA-THUNK!
ROOOOAAAAARRRR!
poop!

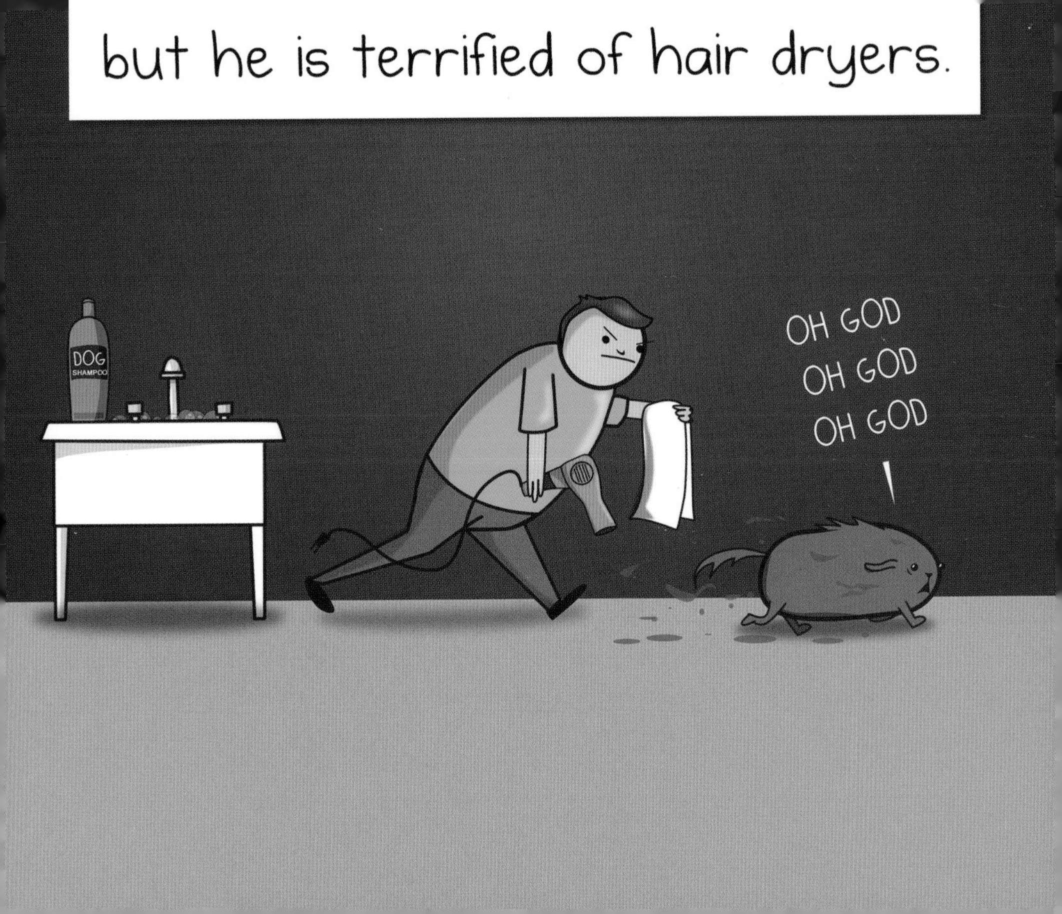
but he is terrified of hair dryers.
DOG SHAMPOO
OH GOD
OH GOD
OH GOD

He does not fear bears, moose, or other dangerous fauna

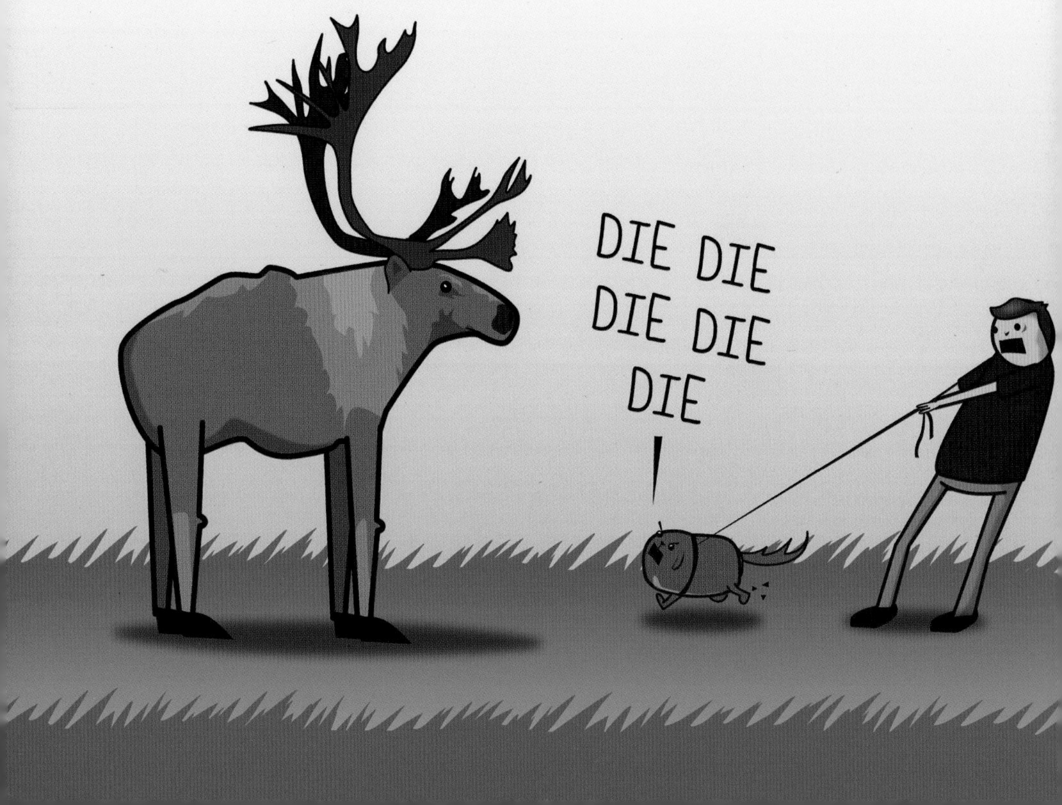
DIE DIE DIE DIE DIE

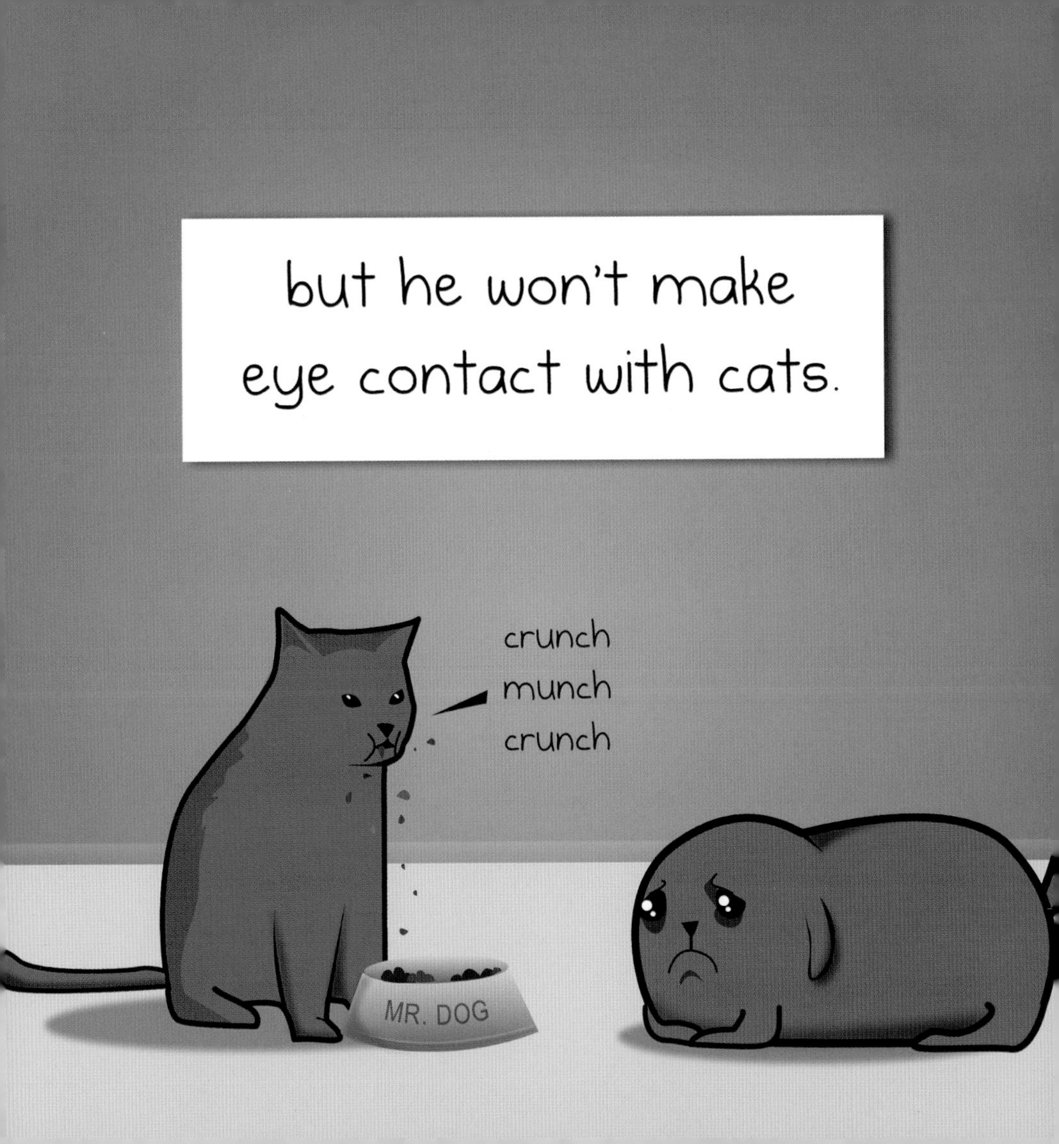
but he won't make eye contact with cats.
crunch
munch
crunch
MR. DOG

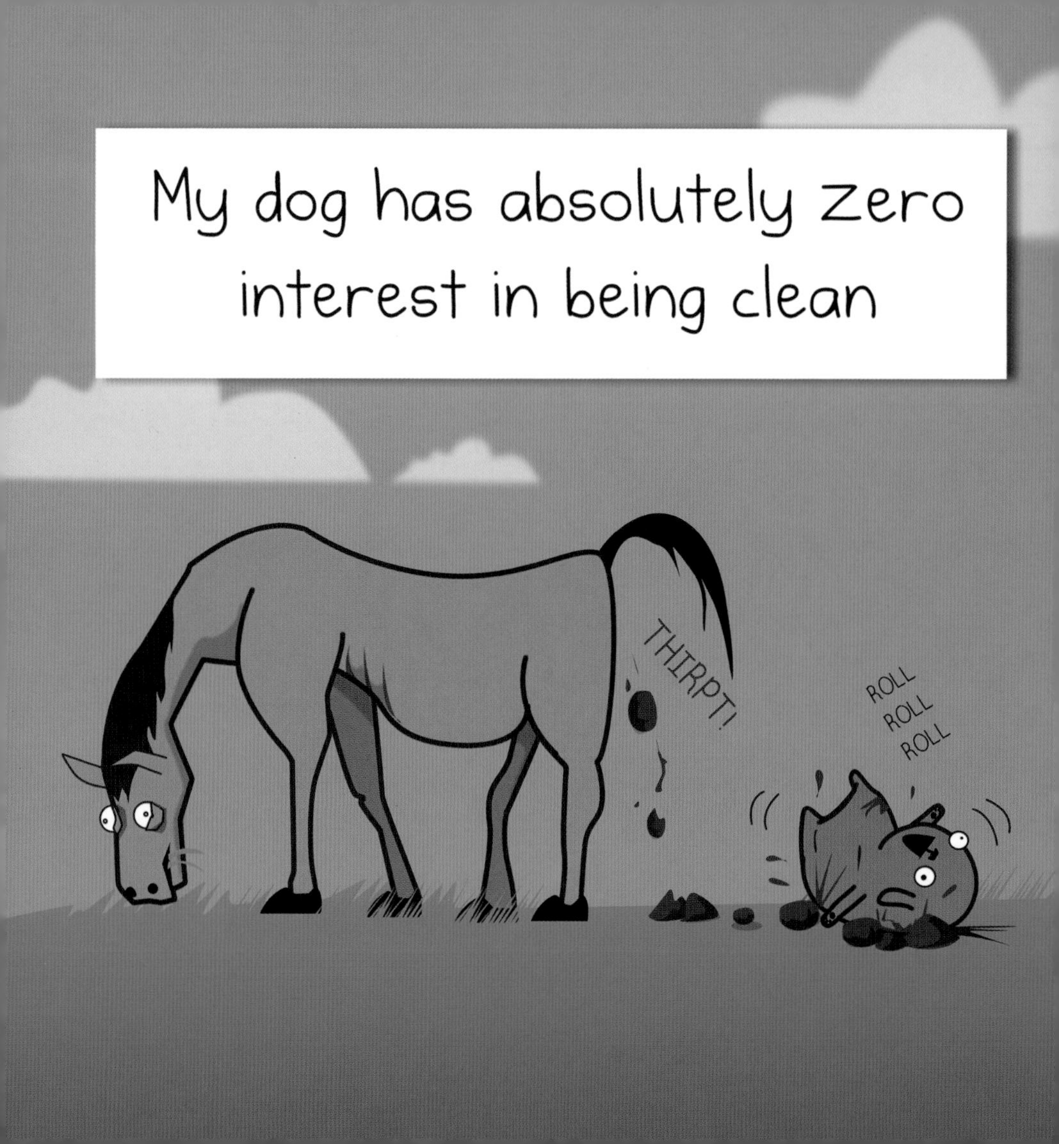
My dog has absolutely zero interest in being clean
THIRPT!
ROLL
ROLL
ROLL

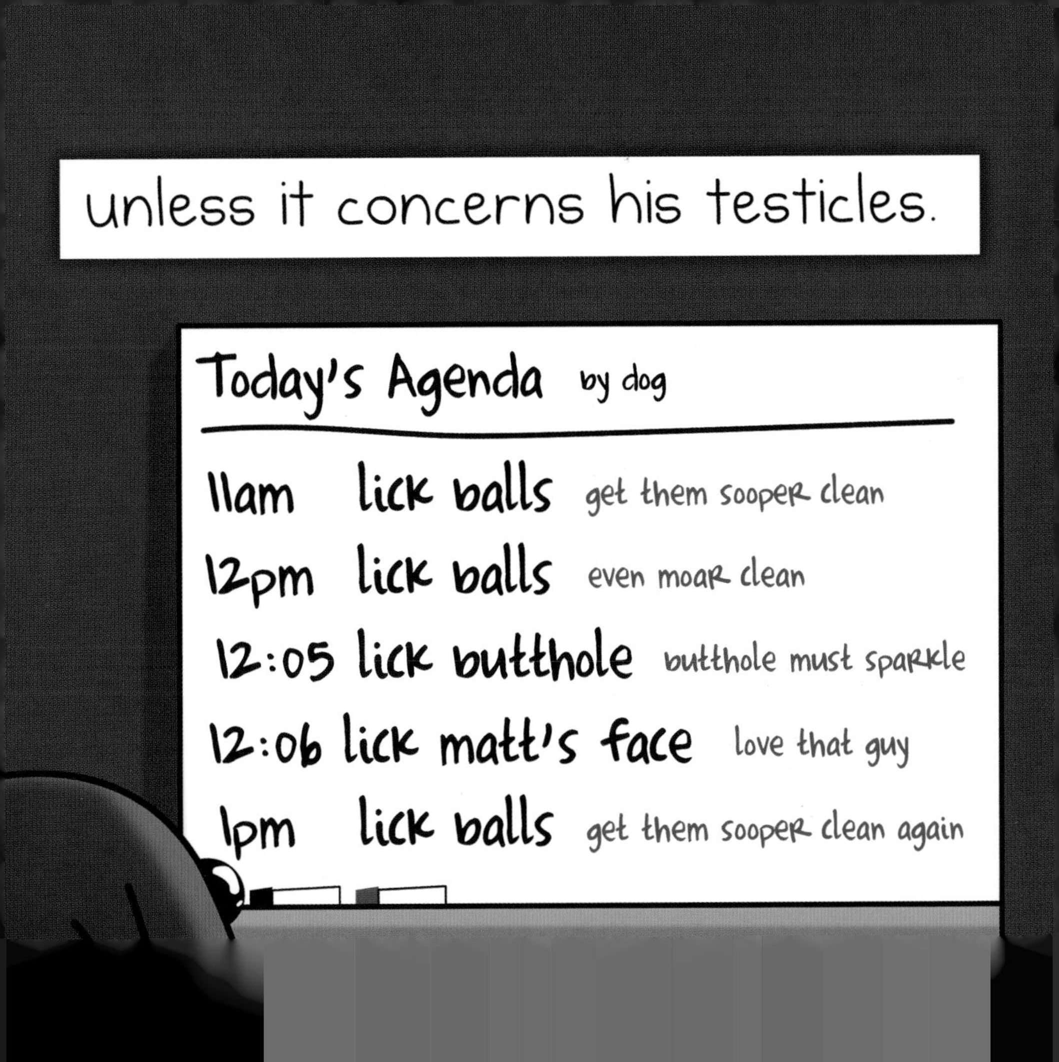

unless it concerns his testicles.

Today's Agenda by dog

11am	lick balls	get them sooper clean
12pm	lick balls	even moar clean
12:05	lick butthole	butthole must sparkle
12:06	lick matt's face	love that guy
1pm	lick balls	get them sooper clean again

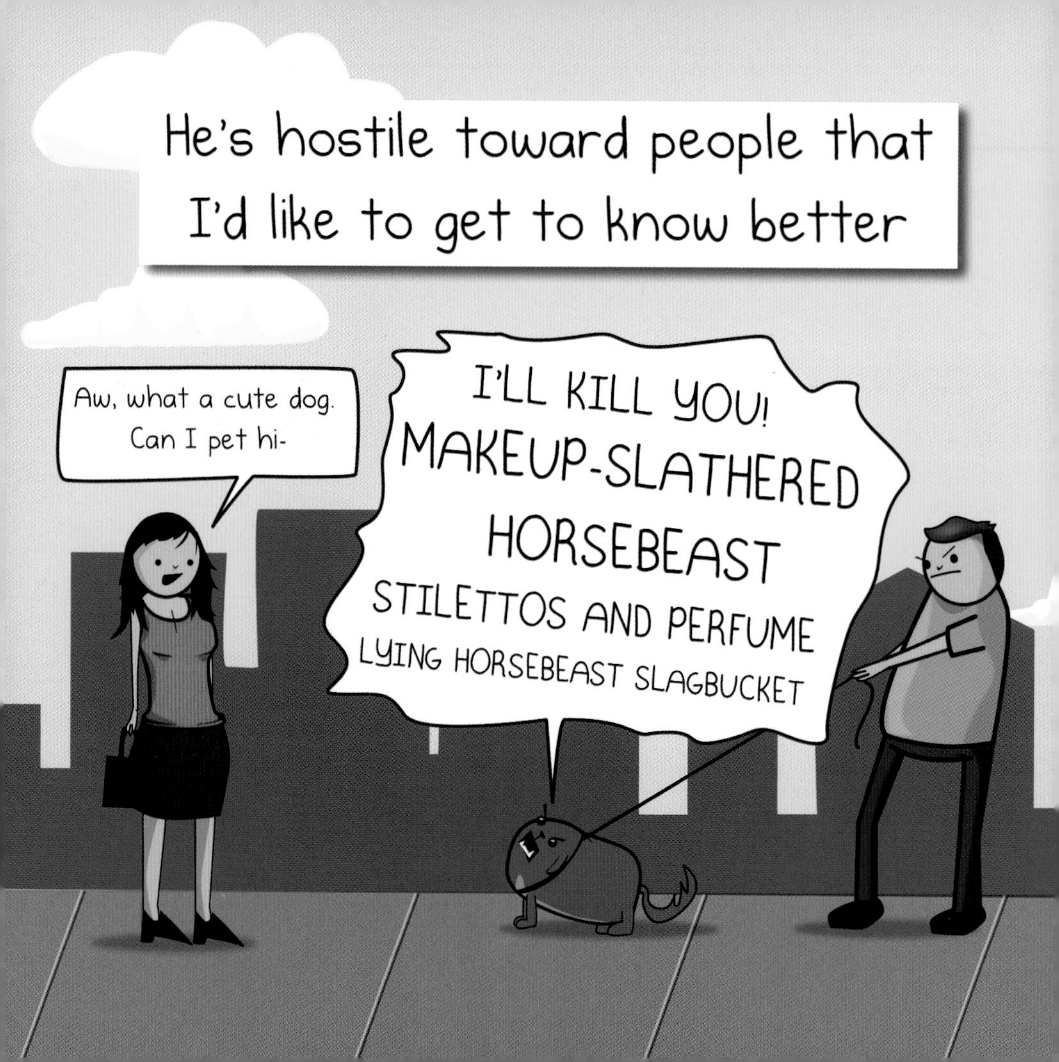
He's hostile toward people that I'd like to get to know better
Aw, what a cute dog. Can I pet hi-
I'LL KILL YOU! MAKEUP-SLATHERED HORSEBEAST STILETTOS AND PERFUME LYING HORSEBEAST SLAGBUCKET

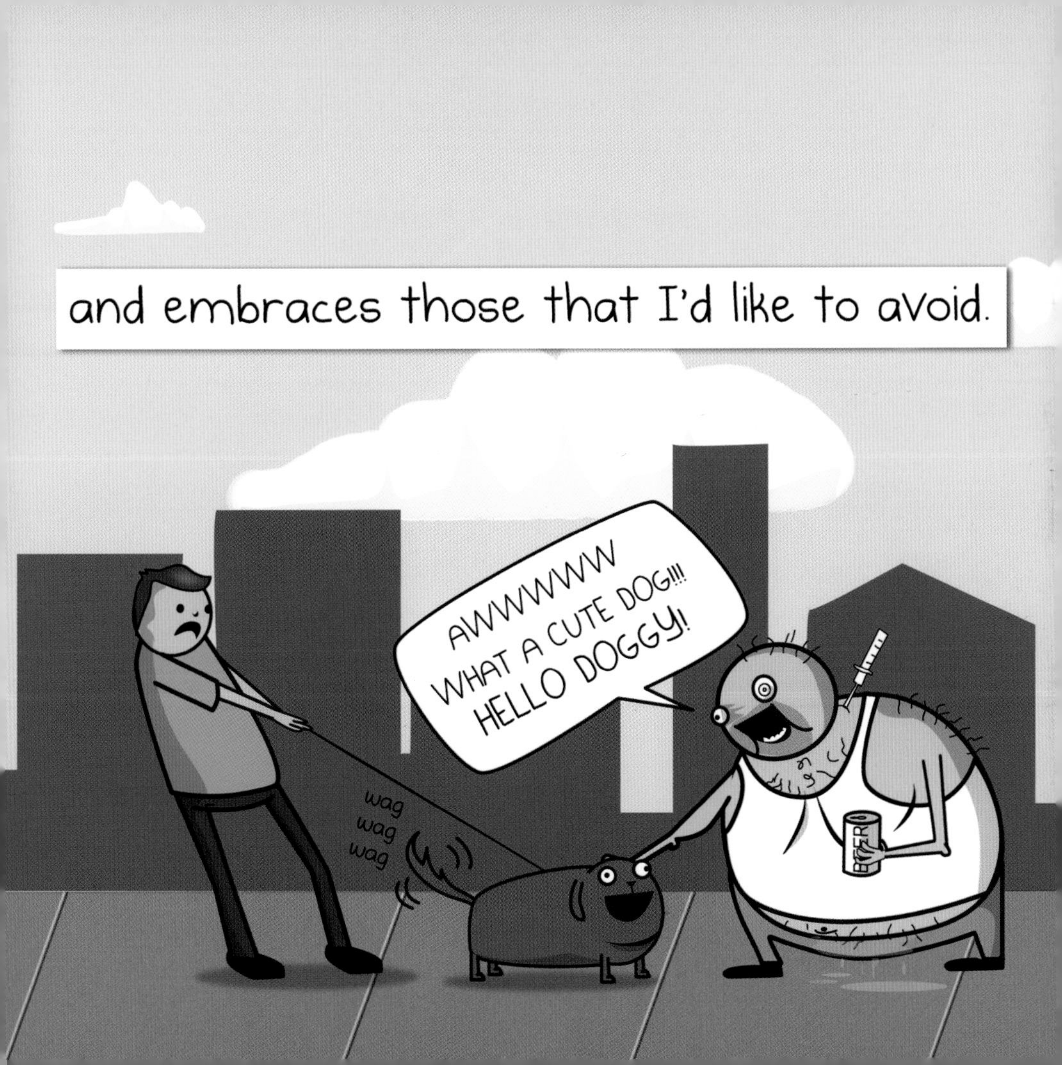
and embraces those that I'd like to avoid.
AWWWWWW WHAT A CUTE DOG!!! HELLO DOGGY!
wag wag wag

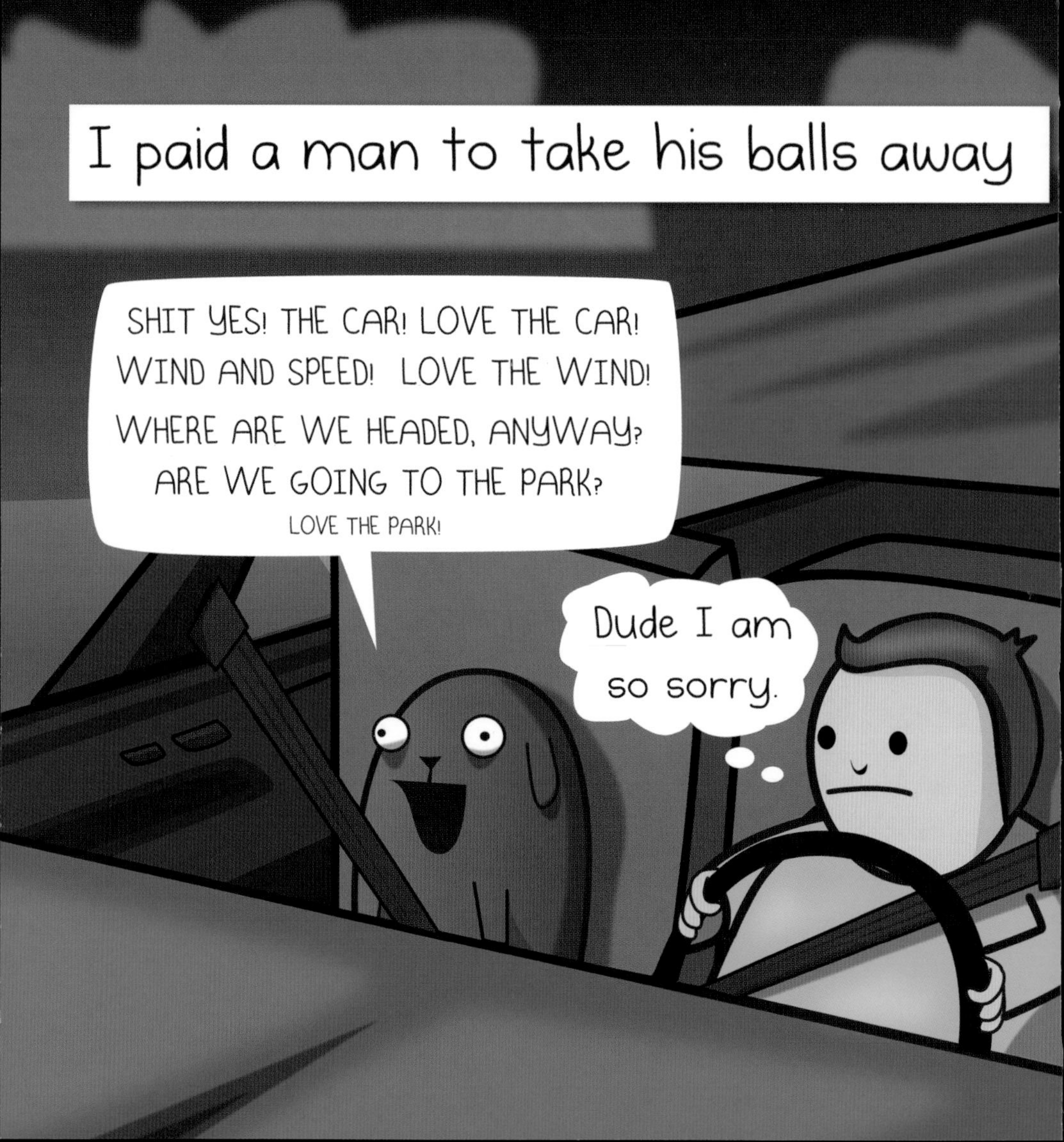
I paid a man to take his balls away
SHIT YES! THE CAR! LOVE THE CAR! WIND AND SPEED! LOVE THE WIND! WHERE ARE WE HEADED, ANYWAY? ARE WE GOING TO THE PARK? LOVE THE PARK!
Dude I am so sorry.

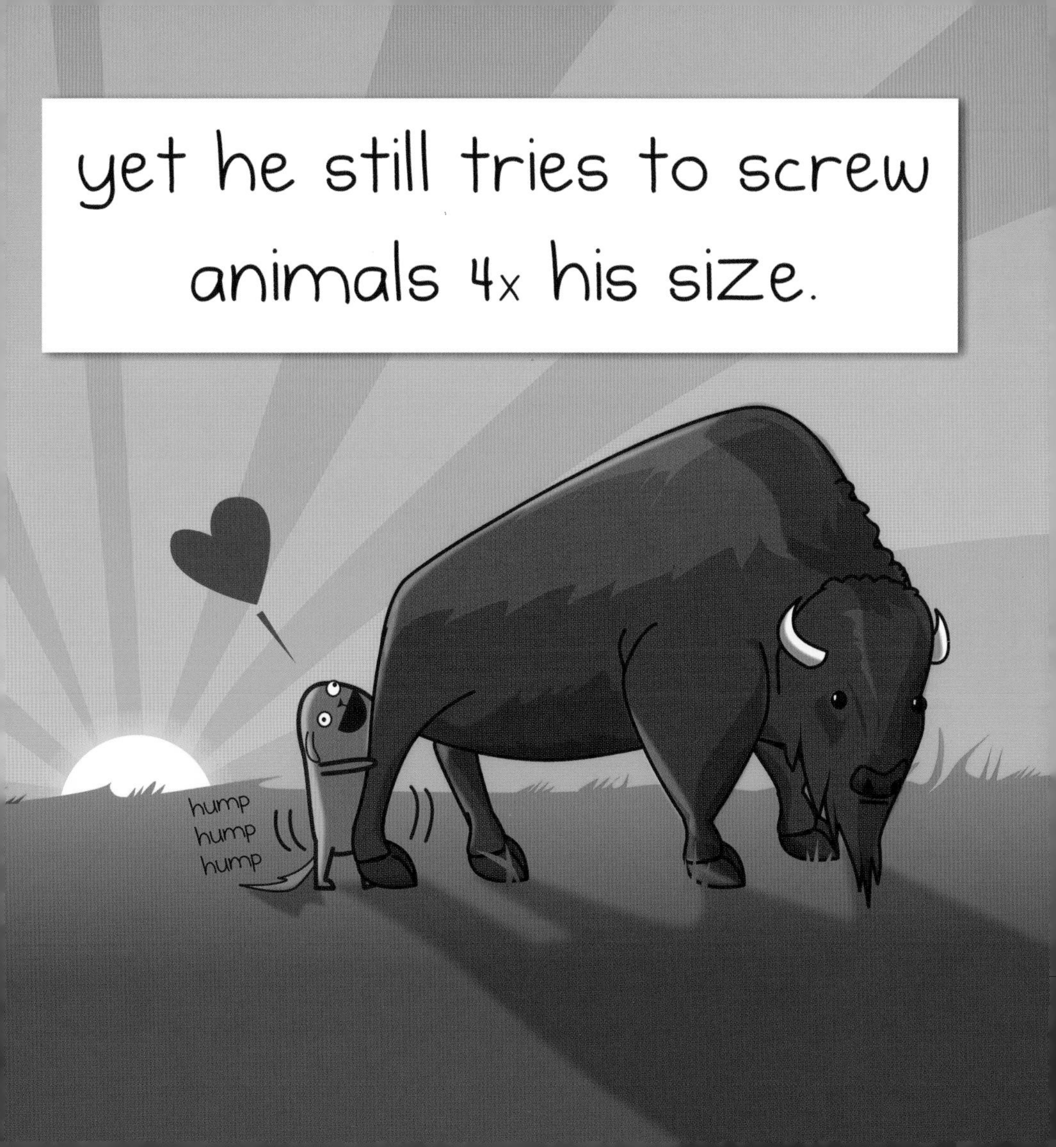
yet he still tries to screw animals 4x his size.
hump hump hump

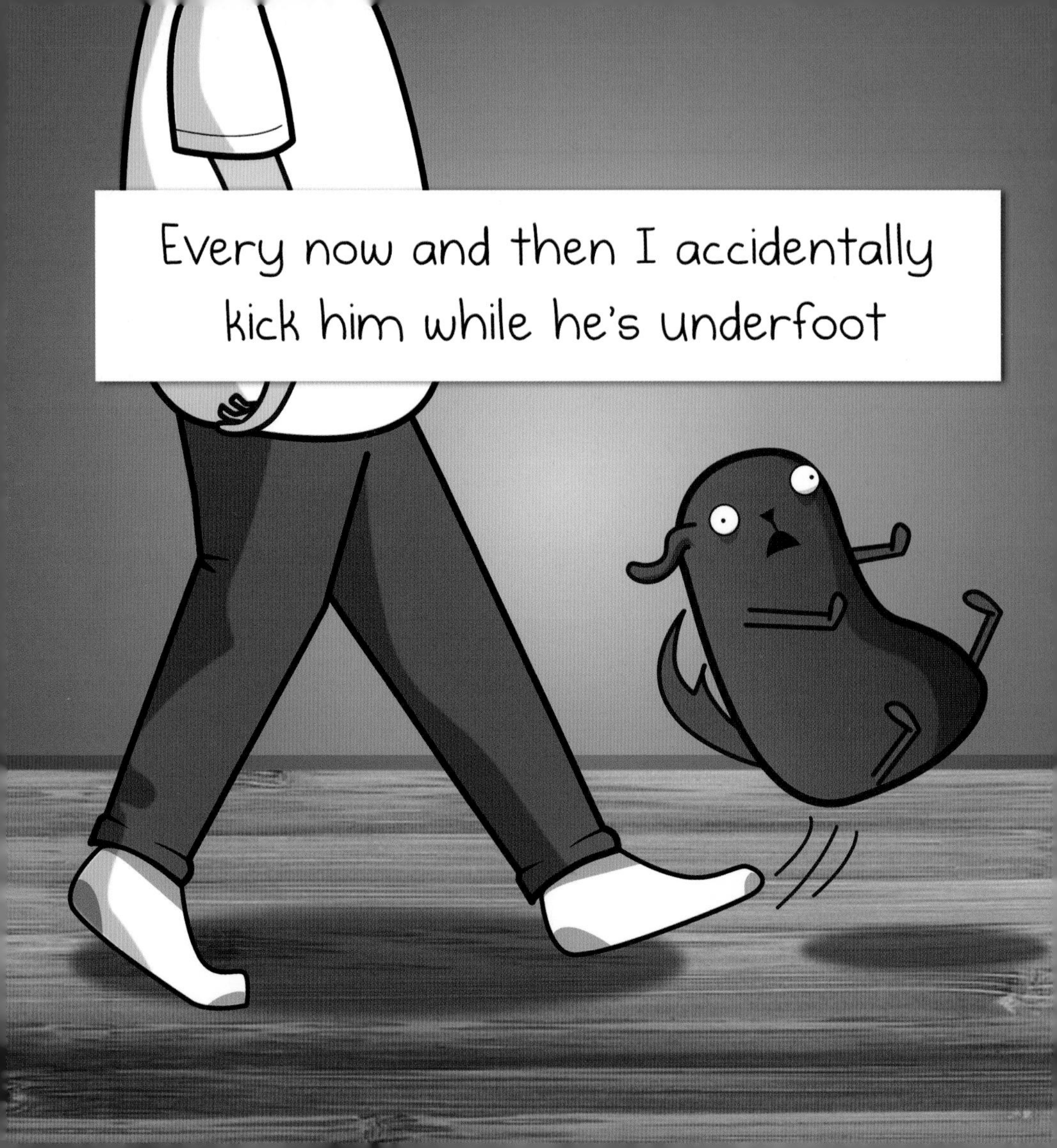
Every now and then I accidentally kick him while he's underfoot

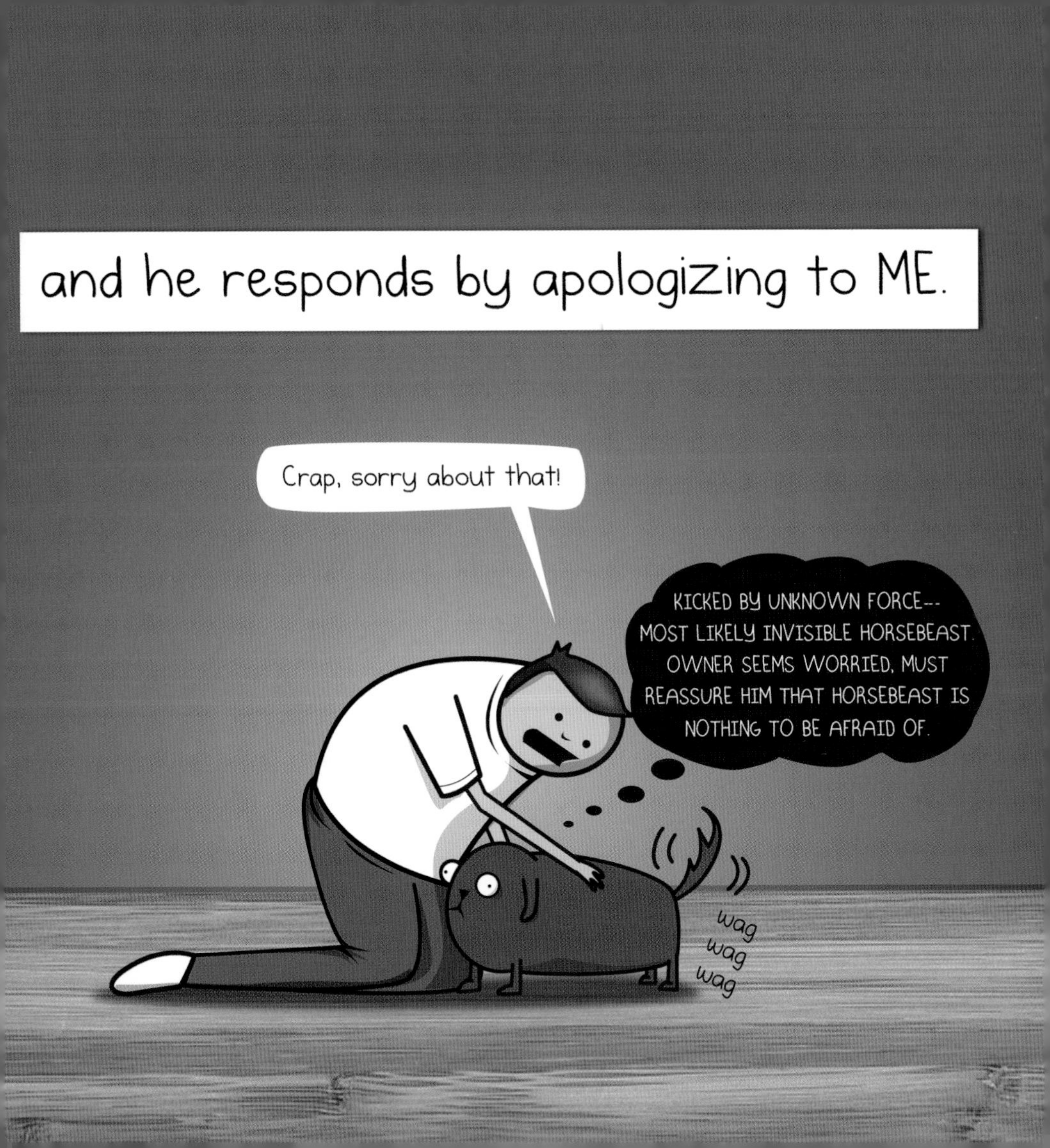
and he responds by apologiZing to ME.
Crap, sorry about that!
KICKED BY UNKNOWN FORCE-- MOST LIKELY INVISIBLE HORSEBEAST. OWNER SEEMS WORRIED, MUST REASSURE HIM THAT HORSEBEAST IS NOTHING TO BE AFRAID OF.
wag wag wag

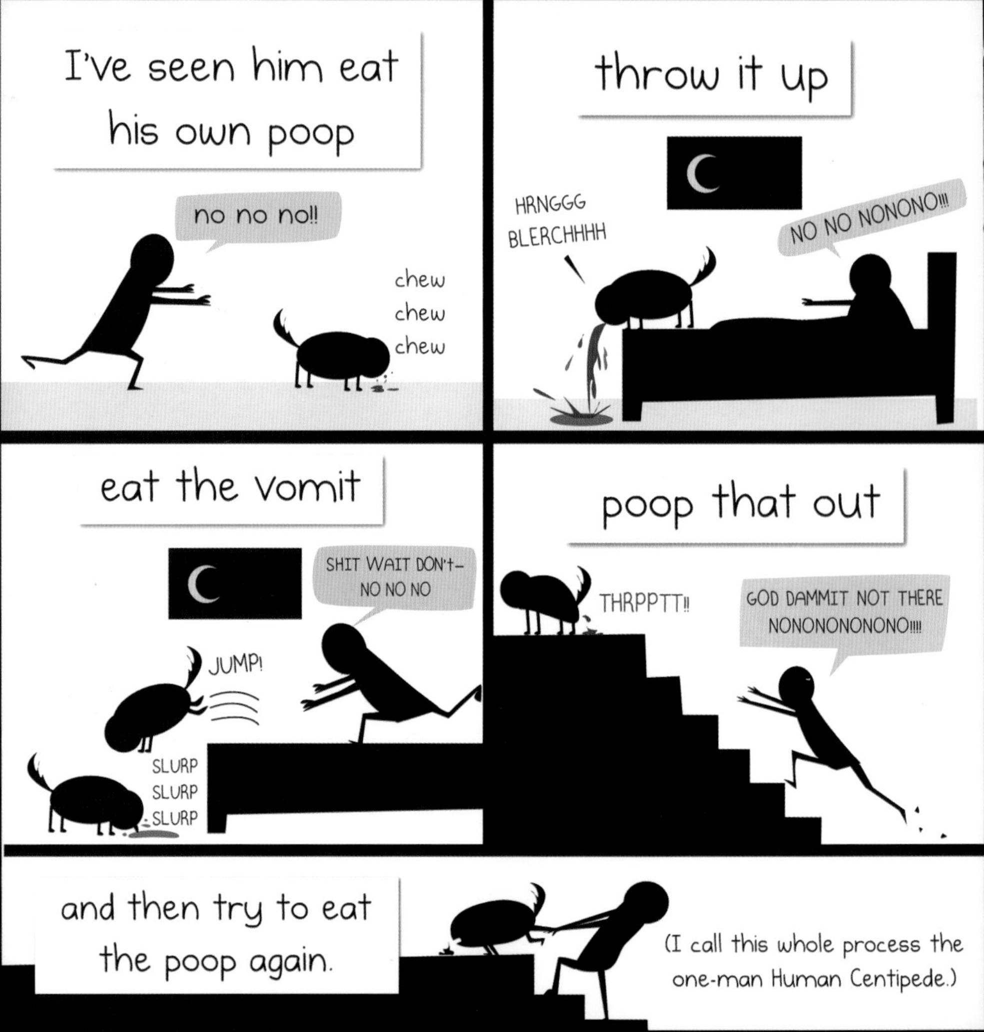
I've seen him eat his own poop
no no no!!
chew
chew
chew
throw it up
HRNGGG
BLERCHHHH
NO NO NONONO!!!
eat the vomit
SHIT WAIT DON't–
NO NO NO
JUMP!
SLURP
SLURP
SLURP
poop that out
THRPPTT!!
GOD DAMMIT NOT THERE
NONONONONONO!!!!
and then try to eat the poop again.
(I call this whole process the one-man Human Centipede.)

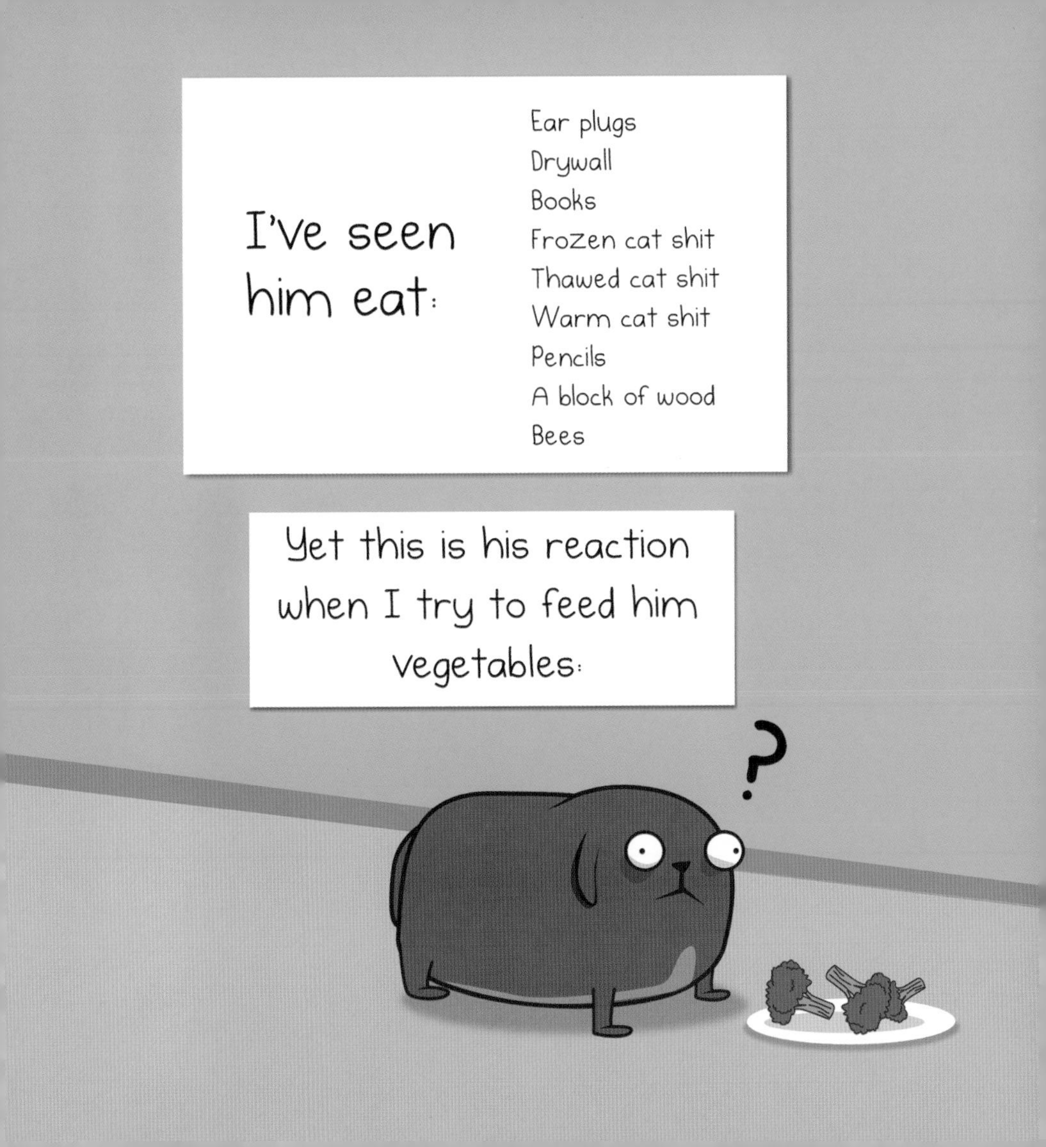
I've seen him eat:
Ear plugs
Drywall
Books
Frozen cat shit
Thawed cat shit
Warm cat shit
Pencils
A block of wood
Bees
Yet this is his reaction when I try to feed him vegetables:
?

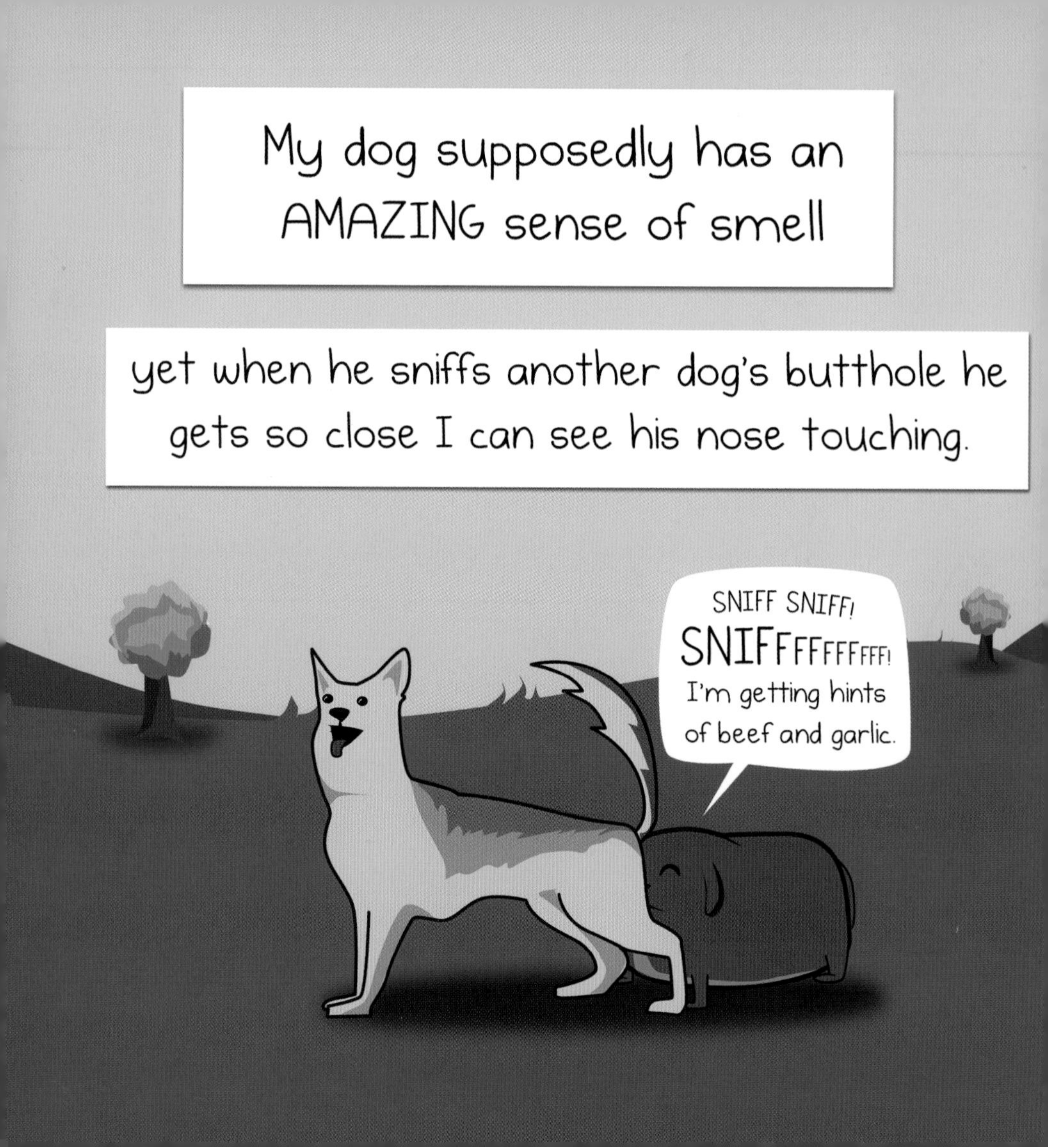
My dog supposedly has an AMAZING sense of smell
yet when he sniffs another dog's butthole he gets so close I can see his nose touching.
SNIFF SNIFF! SNIFFFFFFFFFF! I'm getting hints of beef and garlic.

If his sense of smell is so powerful, couldn't he do that from 20 feet away?

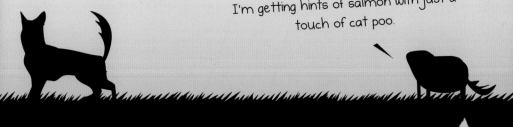

SNIFF SNIFF SNIFFFFFFFF!
What a wonderful bouquet!
I'm getting hints of salmon with just a
touch of cat poo.

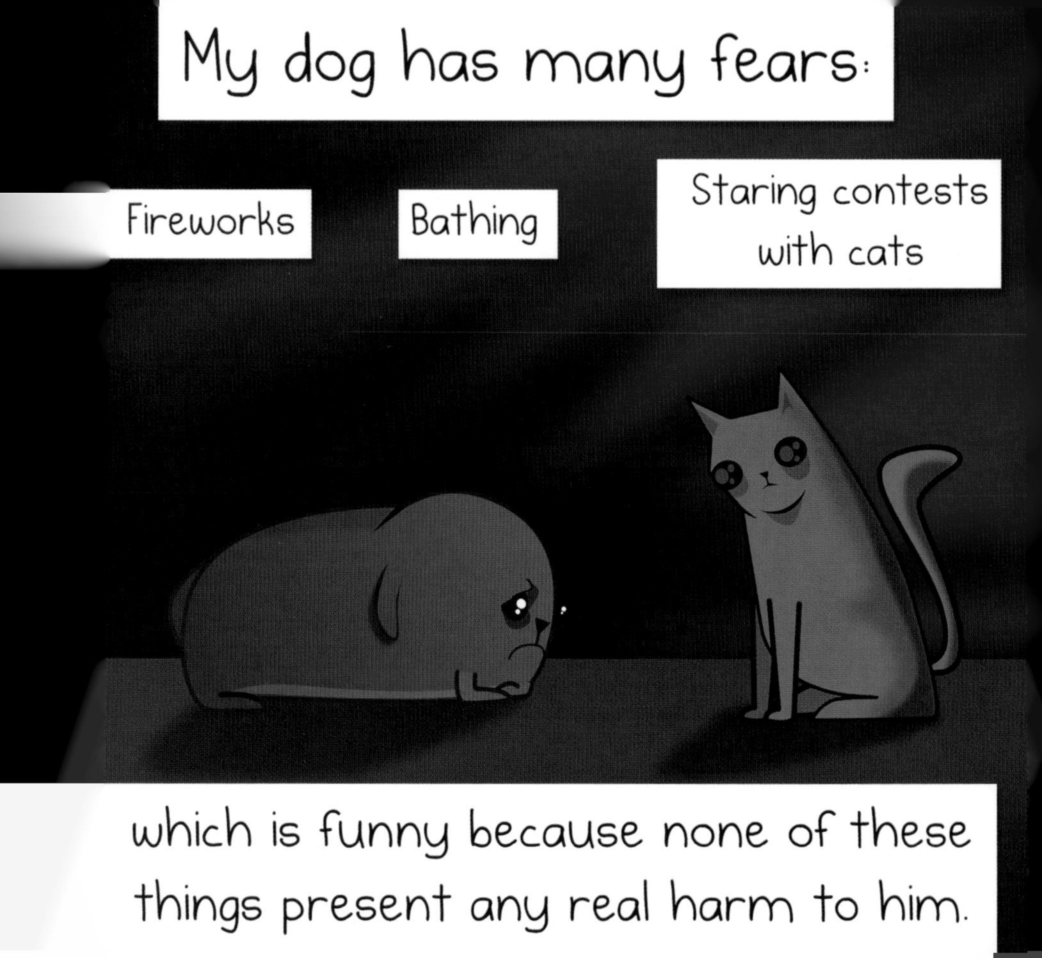
My dog has many fears:
Fireworks
Bathing
Staring contests with cats
which is funny because none of these things present any real harm to him.

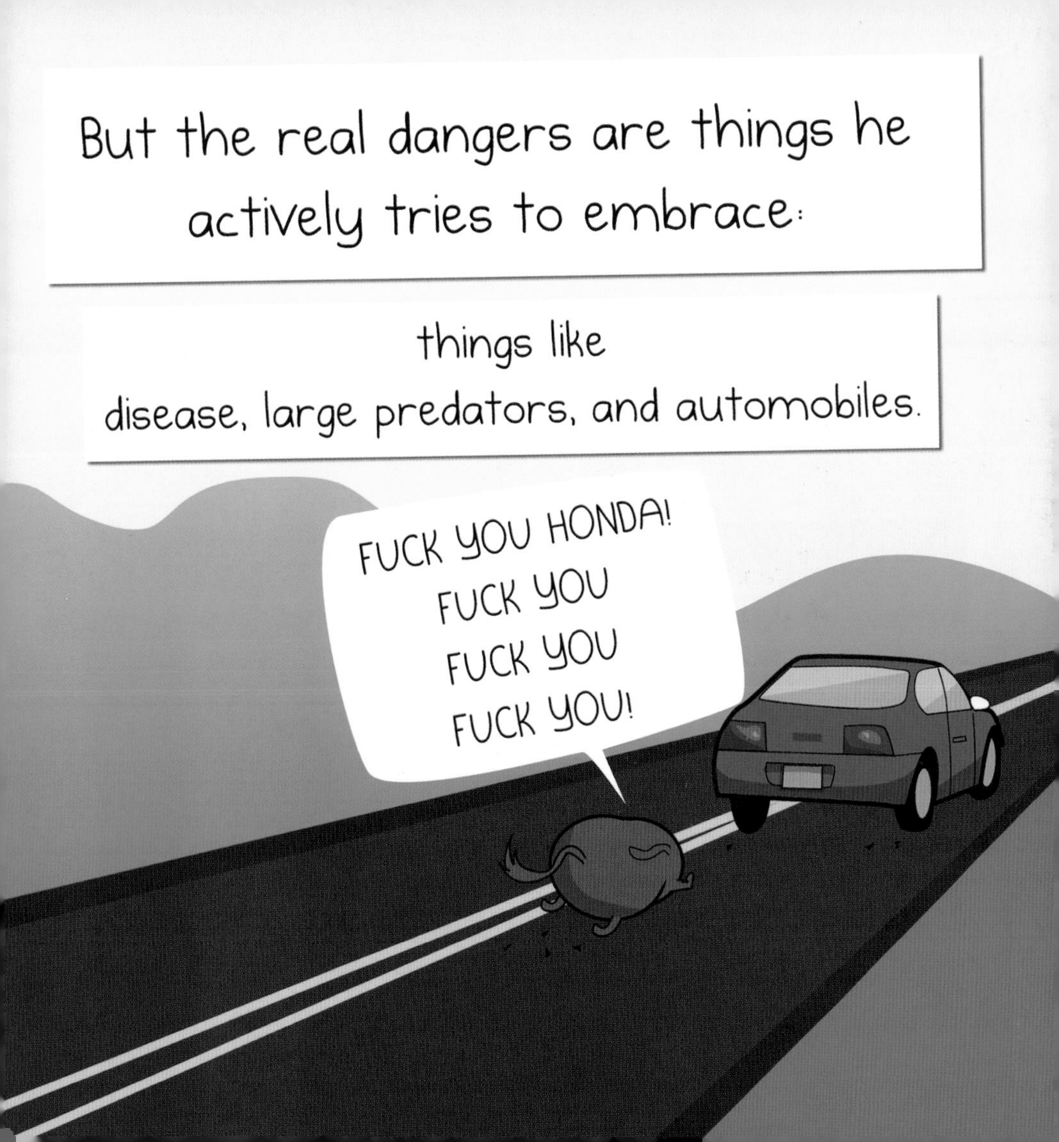
But the real dangers are things he actively tries to embrace:
things like disease, large predators, and automobiles.
FUCK YOU HONDA! FUCK YOU FUCK YOU FUCK YOU!

My dog's biggest fear, however, is

being alone

because every time I come home he acts like he hasn't seen me in decades.

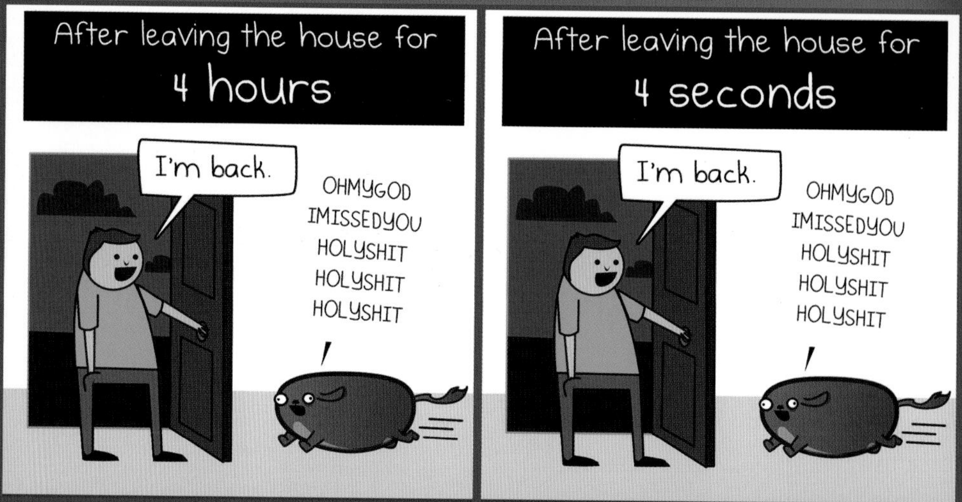
After leaving the house for 4 hours
I'm back.
OHMYGOD IMISSEDYOU HOLYSHIT HOLYSHIT HOLYSHIT
After leaving the house for 4 seconds
I'm back.
OHMYGOD IMISSEDYOU HOLYSHIT HOLYSHIT HOLYSHIT

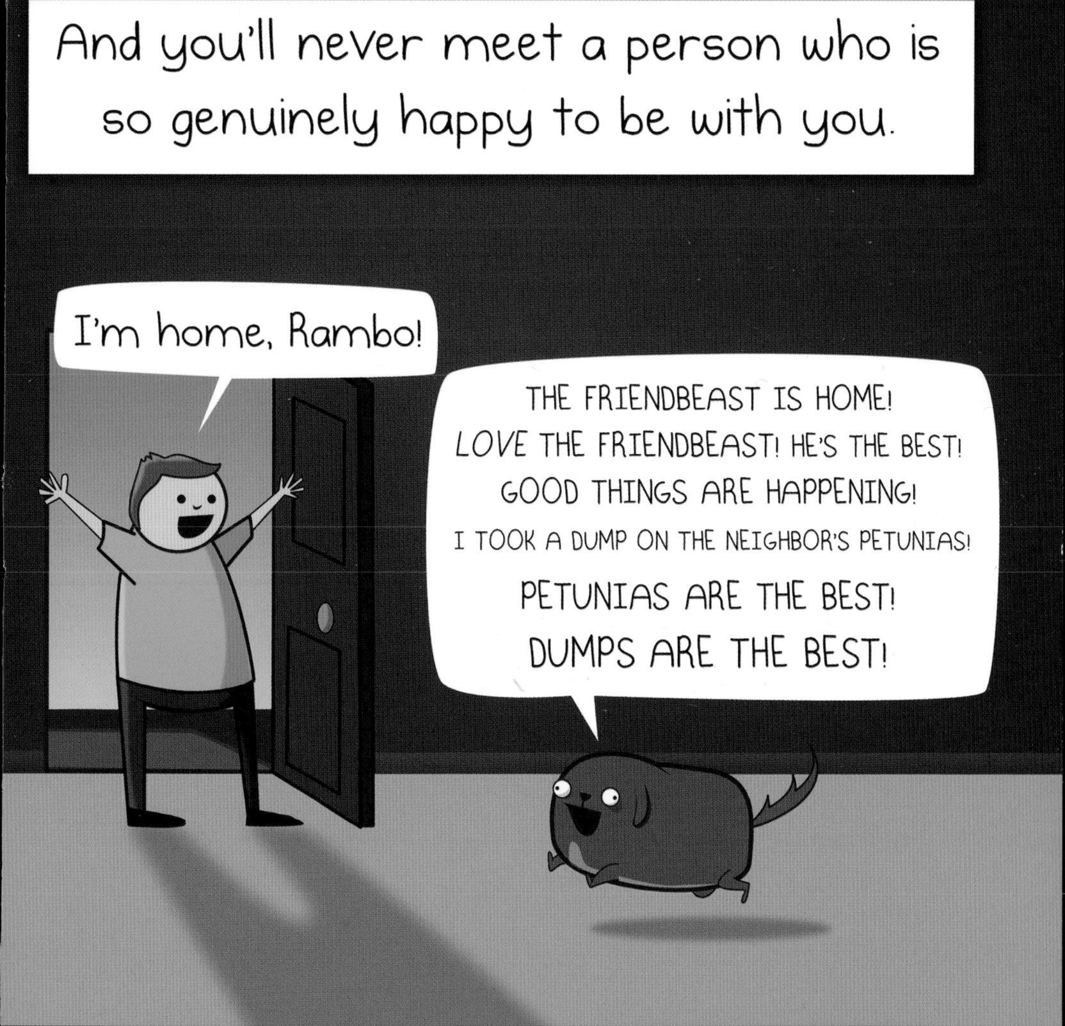
And you'll never meet a person who is so genuinely happy to be with you.
I'm home, Rambo!
THE FRIENDBEAST IS HOME! *LOVE* THE FRIENDBEAST! HE'S THE BEST! GOOD THINGS ARE HAPPENING! I TOOK A DUMP ON THE NEIGHBOR'S PETUNIAS! PETUNIAS ARE THE BEST! DUMPS ARE THE BEST!

THE END!

Dedicated to Rambo.
May he live a thousand years.

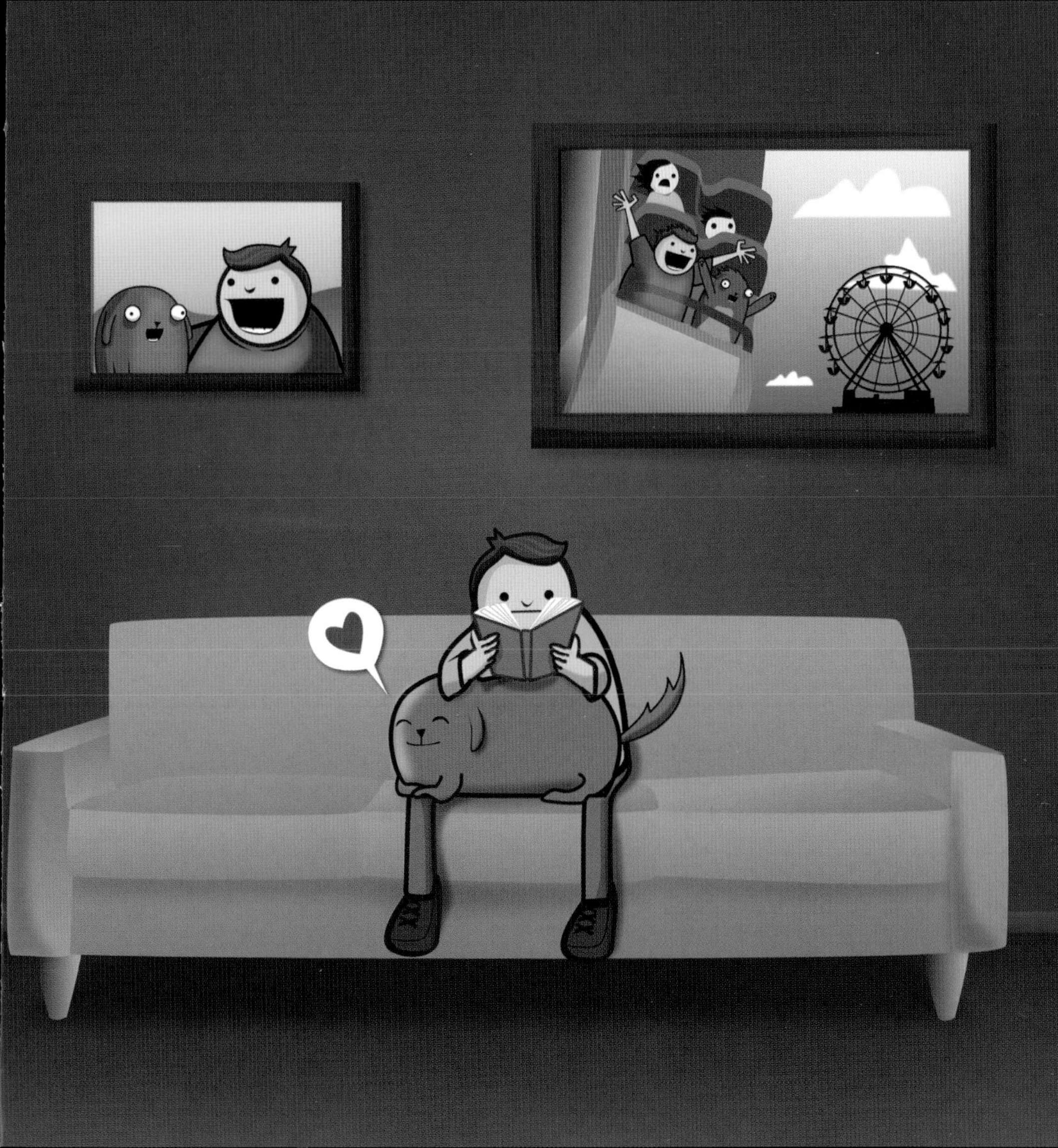

Andrews McMeel Publishing, LLC
an Andrews McMeel Universal company
1130 Walnut Street, Kansas City, Missouri 64106

www.andrewsmcmeel.com

13 14 15 16 17 SDB 10 9 8 7 6 5 4 3

ISBN: 978-1-4494-3752-7

ATTENTION: SCHOOLS AND BUSINESSES
Andrews McMeel books are available at quantity discounts with bulk purchase for educational, business, or sales promotional use. For information, please e-mail the Andrews McMeel Publishing Special Sales Department:
specialsales@amuniversal.com